Just This

Poems of Freedom

Avigail Graetz

BookLeaf Publishing

India | USA | UK

Presentation by *BookLeaf Publishing*

Web: www.bookleafpub.com

E-mail: info@bookleafpub.com

ISBN: 9789363315952

First edition 2024

DEDICATION

Dedicated to all the people that their lives were shattered from October 7th, 2024 on all sides; Israel, Gaza, Palestine and around the world.

Dedicated to Yonatan Amir Itzhaki who died in the age of 20 from cancer on October 11th, 2024. I had the privilege to accompany him in his last year with the support of the Buddha's way. Near his deathbed, there was a small picture of a rat wearing the symbol of peace holding a sign "Get out while you can". I hear it as a liberating call. May his memory be a reminder to let compassion rap and hold us in every moment. Just because we humans can.

I pray for the health of my beloved aunt Menorah Rotenberg who always thought I was possible.

To my Dharma teacher Yonatan Dominitz and my friends Noga Klinger and Tali Meirson. Meeting them and their astonishingly different ways of dealing with cancer is an immeasurable inspiration to live an awakened life.

PREFACE

Writing was always a part of my life, a tool that enabled me to express joy and frustration, anger and anticipation, my sense of astonishment and awe from things, and my craving to be understood in a world that I sometimes could not figure out. I came from a religious home in a secular community, my parents were Americans who moved to Israel, and if these major differences were not enough, I was the tallest girl in the whole school. Always. So writing was and still is a refuge for me. Throughout the years, I studied film, literature and wrote screenplays, theater plays, poems and even a family novel. It's such a joy when your words meet their audience, like looking in the eyes of someone who loves you.

A bit before my 29th birthday, I went to my first silent Vipassana meditation retreat, not knowing it will be the first of many, that it will become my path, my passion and literally a way of living that saved my life and keeps saving it on a daily basis.

The poems in this book were mostly written in a very dark time for me. On October 7th while I was getting ready to teach a day-long meditation workshop about the power of joy we have and should apply more often, sirens were heard in

Tel Aviv. A violent war had started, and as I write these words in May 2024 it is still going on. My life partner and I were always peace activists, we engaged the Dharma, the Buddha's teaching in our daily life, opposing the Israeli occupation, calling for peace, making Palestinian friends and trying to change the Israeli way of looking through our films and actions.

Within days when it was clear to us that our country was turning stronger and stronger towards war and the fear for our one child's safety grew we decided to flee for Greece. I continued supporting my Buddhist community through Zoom, in fact, even on October 7th and the days to follow, Israel's Insight Meditation Society, where I have taught for many years, had 3 sessions a day of Zoom meetings for relaxing and creating a bigger space in the heart, mind and body to contain the horrific state we were all experiencing. This continued for months, and I offered daily Zoom sessions to different crowds, like the medical staff of a big hospital, young mothers, reserved forces and whoever was in need.

We came home after two and a half months for a one-month stay and continued to India where a true shelter was found. Our country and Palestine are suffering tremendously. I could not stay at a place where the hearts of people are hardening so strongly and the voice of peace is boycotted and not legitimate. It will take a long time to heal and much letting go is needed on both sides. I am willing to pay the price of my actions. The Buddhist way that prays for equality and respect of precious human life for all is my compass. I hope the poems express that and encourage people to seek freedom in every moment.

I don't know what the future holds, we never do, but the ability to put the right intention in every step, action and word is definitely up to us. We are working on a documentary that is titled- "Where Is Home". I'm happy I follow the Buddha's teaching that calls us to be an island to ourselves. An island that is connected to all of life with threads that are sometimes in the dark, but with one compassionate look able to reveal beauty, harmony and grace that hold us all, that give us home right here, right now, in just this moment.

Chasing Peace

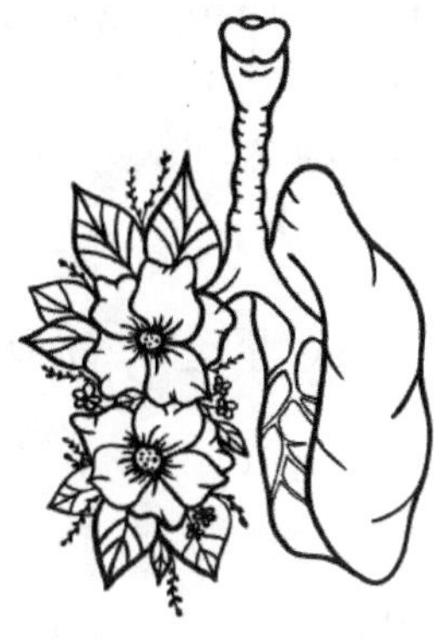

What can an Israeli woman do in 2024
While she chooses to stay away from her
homeland?

Hug the middle line of the body.
Support from afar,
Trust she is at the accurate distance.

Tremble together with the pain that comes
through
Zoom windows or from people full of sorrow
that fled.
That stayed.

Guiding meditation that reminds people of
softness,

of the seed of freedom that is planted within
them.
Oppose the war even against those who support
her country,
Smile in disagreement to those who think
completely differently.
Smile truly.
Remember that everything is transient and
changes.
Everything.

Strengthen the body,
Cry out with mothers, who oppose the war,
Pray for freedom for both sides sake.

Agree to be part of humankind;
Sad, angry, hurt, helpless and not knowing.
Choose to be a seeker of peace and freedom
under all conditions.
Ask for peace and chase it wherever she goes.

Stay creative even with writing one kind word or
taking a conscious step that kisses the earth.

Hug the middle line of the body.
It is home.

Taking refuge

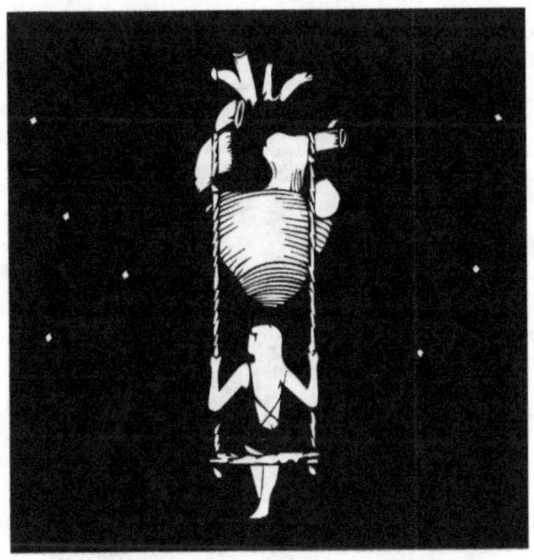

Taking refuge in the world,
In this vast moment I cannot grasp.
My Indian landlords are making a fire in their
backyard
near our laundry.
Every garment that flutters in an attempt to dry
was created in a different part of the world that
does not have a lord.
Only this moment I can smell, touch, hear, see,
think and taste is under my control.
The party is always inside us.
Just this is my refuge.

The illusion of stillness

The Buddha's right way to talk,
The language, the movement, the thought.
It is not possible to hide the blood cells
like hiding the Hebrew by taking the other side
of the notebook to write in English.
Like taking the other side of the sidewalk to hide
fear.
Movement cannot be hidden,
It's all so shaky even when we feel it is all still.
It is always moving like earth.
The illusion of stillness like the
Buddha's stickers
showing only his face, his calm head,
not his full body

strengthening the illusion,
he tried to shatter over and over;
There is a body.
This body will age, get sick and die.
And that's okay
Deeply okay
It's all about feeling the feeling within the
feeling,
surrendering to movement with deep calmness.

The Grace of the Spirit

A thread of grace is stretched
from the meadow of the Israeli Kibbutz
I reached 20 years ago for my first silent retreat
mediation
all the way to
the lawn of the Thai monastery in Bodhgaya,
India.
And every word, object, organ and concept in
me and
in the opening sentence changed,
But the wind blowing from the monastery
all the way back
to my suffering land-
The wind whispering freedom.

17/4/2024

On my daughter's birthday
A butterfly visits my porch.
I write my porch even though
It's a temporary house in India
I'm staying at as my country is a war zone.
I write my country even though
I am a Buddhist that knows suffering arises
From attaching to
Me, Mine, Myself.
This beautiful visit of the flickering butterfly
now resting before me is a gentle reminder
that my daughter belongs to the world.
Just like him she's entitled to land wherever she
chooses.

Tea Time

Drinking Chai on the Indian porch
watching tall slim coconut trees standing
like birthday candles, no one can blow out,
reminding me of all those years
I was blaming myself
being too tall to be loved.

A crow passes by demonstrates its blackness
landing on the white balcony,
maybe frustrated the coconut trees can't
host it,
Perhaps just manifesting colors.

Cheery squirrels hopping on
lower trees in the yard
not bothered where they can or cannot travel
reminding me of the middle-way path I choose
that taught me
there is no problem with my tallness,
with life.
I am a tall woman gladly drinking tea.
No struggle is needed.

May Day in South Goa: Inspiration at the Chai Shop

The charm of the Chai Shop
Is like a time tunnel.
I remember waiting for it to open
at five A.M with my two-year-old baby that
woke up
at four A.M as if she were a Buddhist nun up for
her morning meditation.

Nine years have passed
I return to my personal time tunnel
to play cards with my blooming daughter.
Nothing and everything changed.

The same empty Baji pot
still spreads spices,
The refrigerator now with a sticker of a
flying rickshaw,
Krishna and Buddha in their places
and a new 'No digital pay' sign.

Three sons constantly busy,
their father that used to open the door for me
at dawn had just died.
My own father is towards the end of his life
opened all the doors in the world for me
teaching me to live life well, live it mighty
as God is everywhere.

I feel him call my name.

The floor full of dust and stains,
imitating the holy ground
calls me to get down on my feet and bow.
The white string dangles from the ceiling,
ready to tie with a string
takeaway samosas bundled in fresh newspapers
calls me to raise my hands up with gratitude to
the sky above.

The power's off,
The fan stops,
The heat is immeasurable,
Yet there is no place on earth I would rather be.
The Chai Shop is a temple.

Nature is Home

Morning time in Goa
so far away from home.
Nature is celebrating before me
providing a sense of home
with every breath I share with it.

One insistent butterfly on a nearby branch does
not let go,
her friend rushes past me,
but she patiently stays near me.
Squirrels climbing up and down,
A dog wanders,
crows fly with their peculiar sounds.
A monkey appears like the king of the jungle,
first rests near the high-water tank tower

observing the yard, the old well,
thinking-
I choose not to evolve like humans
so desperate to guard and control water,
the world.

He continues his stroll between the trees,
lands gracefully on the red roof of humans.
I too take the challenge of writing in my
mother's tongue,
I step out of my comfort zone questioning
without words- where is home.
Nature is doing its dance regardless of both
our efforts.

The Indian landlord does not want monkeys
roaming around his yard,
hopping on his red rooftop-
Go away you, choose a different path.

He drums on an old silver plate
to chase him away
reminds me the drums of war
that chased us away from home.

We're all in this together.
It's the same dance.
The butterfly is still here
providing a momentary home.

The joy of breath, sounds, colors,
nature is providing all the
nourishment needed.
This joyous morning- Good enough shelter.

Freedom is a human possibility

They say when I was little
I asked when will I be possible.
More than forty years later I still shiver thinking
How sad it must have been to hear
I am impossible.

Now I shake my body, my bones, my blood
Knowing "Todo Es Possible" not only in fluent
Spanish but in every cell of my
body-mind-heart.

Beautiful Mess

In my daughter's room
I lay on her bed
watch the mess piled up
everywhere I lay my eyes.

No Mary Poppins in sight
No capable mother who can organize.
Only written words can save us.
Like the saying on her shirt thrown on the floor
"Queen".
I focus my eyes on the tidiness she drew
in a Zen painting.
So distant from the door I used to slam
behind my messy childhood room.

Only crowning this as the most
beautiful mess ever,
the "fairest",
can rescue me.

Take a walk to Deep Okayness

Taking your overwhelmingness from life for a
walk.
Letting it learn your footsteps instead of
you running away from it.

Letting you wash under it all
with every step touching the ground.

Directly experiencing every step,
Directly knowing;
So many
Miracles have happened for this moment,
this floody moment to be as it is.
Walking it through.

Being overwhelmed is a true honor
like our authentic head coming out
under the imaginary helmet we wear
all over.
All the time.
With no need.
Let it be.

Taking the veil off of that which supports us
A mere breath that can liberate the heart and
mind.
Just by noticing it.
Letting it be.

Even a broken heart is an invitation to enjoy it
while it lasts,
soon people will use black heart emojis
you will be so sad the tears are
not available for you.

Cry your overwhelmed tired heart out
Let it rest in every step of deep okayness.

Love and Death

From time to time
Fear of death arises.
I hold a prayer we paid the price when his
brother died on his way home.
Fragile illusion cannot save us.
I remind myself death is the price of life and
only love is priceless and deathless.
The fear stays for a while and subsides
I embrace the temporary cessation,
the fear,
the illusion and death.

The four elements and father

There is nowhere to go and nowhere to return-
This is what the war taught me.
My father, on the throne of his demented dignity
answers sadly - but you need to be somewhere.

Here I am father.

Standing with long legs you gave me
who tried to catch up with your inner fire,
I am here.

Feeling solid ground
in an air that protects me
from bad and good spirits,

reflected in the watery eyes of my only daughter.
Waters separate and unites us all.
Skin so thin and vulnerable.
We will all dismantle back to elements.
But not this moment when I can gently
scream—
I am here.

I shall continue to tell her, on every journey
either by choice or from consequences-
Only this.
The four elements of your body are home.
Trust the world and here you are.
Just this moment contains it all.
Just this.

Relinquishment

I Invite Death over for dinner.
Prefer feeling the vulnerability of being human
than the ignorance I had before I became a
mother.
The Thai teacher Ajan Cha asked:
Why do people cry at funerals
instead of crying when a baby is born?
I cried. I Laughed,
and let the unbearable pain melt by crazy joy
after they slit my vagina to enable my daughter
to see the light.

I praised that which is difficult to bear.
Saw the link,
the thread between birth and death
that is woven on one thin line.
This line is going to die.

Some day.
Not today.

We are not dead yet as we enjoy our dinner
With our biggest demon that arrived with us in
the delivery room.
Death will come no matter what.
Why not let it in and not be bound to time.
Why not let it be just the ending of things
of the way things have come to be.

Nothing to cling on

Tell me what I need to learn when I die.
Breathing in
Kissing life
Surrendering to gravity
Breathing out
Thanking life
Surrendering to gravity.
All fears of death come from identifying with
thoughts, opinions, rituals, with the body.
May I feel it is my time to let go.

Sipping freedom

Drinking cold coffee at Karma Café,
Two concepts of West and East meet
on the old sign,
almost melting from the heat in south Goa.
A blend of concepts of misconceptions,
that the mind is so attached to.
Trying to understand and fix,
to make and have the best journey in
life, while life is just a pool we swim in.

I stare at "Way of living" a book's title
on the dusty bookshelf.
Above, "80 Activities For Children"
placed upside down.

Letting go of figuring this out,
letting go of stories like surrendering
to heat or cold,
surrendering to a smiling Indian family of four
passing on one scooter as I notice
3 stickers on the wall- Live, Love, Laugh.
Whole wisdom in front of my eyes
while a yellow butterfly passes by
and always a cow.
A boy riding his bicycle wearing a Messi
football T-shirt
reminding me to let go of number 10,
of any concept, not sewing and stitching
every fragment
that passes by the sense doors.
Letting life happen just like
the trail of ants exploring the café's floor.
I raise my head to notice the ceiling
(Still binary thinking mode)
I see a small window all the way up.
It's woven with metal bars crisscrossing as
saying no way out.
Something is up there, I rise to see-
A small Buddha statue on the left,
A small Ganesh statue on the right.
Right here and now, a window to freedom.

The Necklace

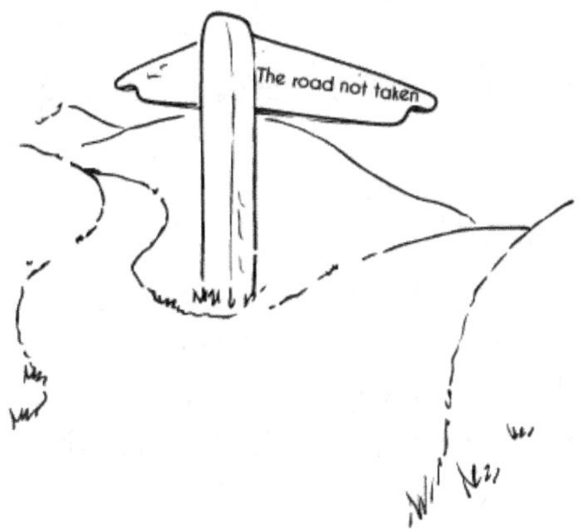

He holds a prayer necklace,
says someone left it behind.
Instead of imagining him in a demolished home
moments before the house explodes,
I think how the beads were probably from
China,
found their way to Gaza
and then taken by him to Israel.

Here at Goa, India
I stare at his thick fingers tossing and turning it
as he does so gracefully with his drums,
with his lover.

He saw it and took it, adding it to his journey.

With or without hesitation.
With or without seeing what and why was it left
behind in the shattered home.

His protection from evil eye now is someone
else's bad luck.
Taking the chain of beads,
the Misbahah, so casually,
taking place in the world.

Was there a moment he could have chosen not to
take it like not buying an Indian Mala that
vendors offer?
Did he save it?
Saved himself?
Did he steal it?
Will his prayers be answered from now on?
Will the house owners in Gaza ever return?
Ever remember these specific ordinary
prayer beads with 99 names of Allah they left
behind?
When will they get a new one and do they still
believe in God?
Who judges cases of destruction,
The choices we make?
Who will heal us all?
Morality knocks all the time,
right or wrong are crumbling in every bead that
goes by.

Math class in times of war

My daughter is learning fractions.
So am I.
In this time of war we all are.

A simple fracture, a simulated fracture,
A fundamental fracture.

How do you find a broken part of a whole?

The most common denominator is birth.
The counter is the time that passes,
Which froze on its fragments on October 7th,
A massive numerator that hovers us all.
We feel like remainders of our old selves.
Like too much was added to our equation.
Like hardship has doubled itself and broke us.

And there is no more suitable time to learn
how to put together what is broken.

To multiply love in the world and to share
suffering and earth under the same sky.
The lesson is-
there is enough for all.

The time that will pass will have to prove
fractures will eventually be reconciled.

A complete fraction, a compound fraction
that plows the furrows of the identity
that clings to roots that cannot be grasped.
We are all broken.
Half-hearted, looking for an eighth solace on the
horizon,
like in the picture that was hanging on the wall
in the old schools.
A farmer, a tractor, landscape.

A sacred moment by the smartphone

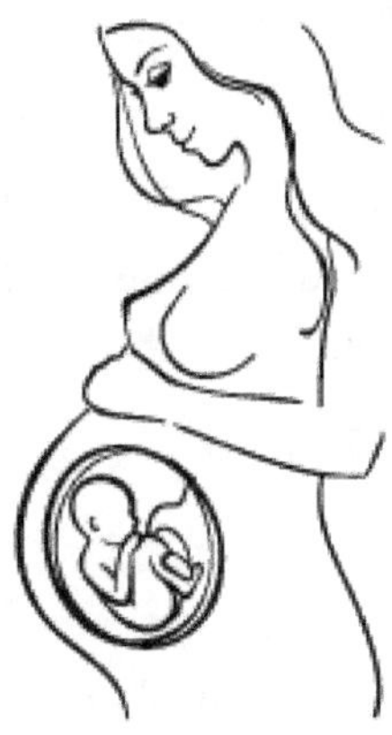

In memory of Yonatan Amir Itzhaki

A sacred moment by the phone
visited by the chills.
They became better known.

A poet sends a daily poem for inspiration
she wonders how her miracles
came about.
How she gave birth to children
out of nowhere
from emptiness.

Suddenly a mother whose son I accompanied to
his death
texts me from the void
asking how I am doing.

How did she accompany him to nowhere
back to emptiness,
only 20 years old?
She sat by him made sure he would not
be frightened from death,
sat by him
as he stopped talking.
Just sat.
That's the big wonder.
That's all there is to write about.

Everything shivers in my fingers
Keep studying the axis of
birth-sickness-old age-death.

Not always in this order.
Always the law of nature.
Intimately sacred. Chilling.

Internal Rotation

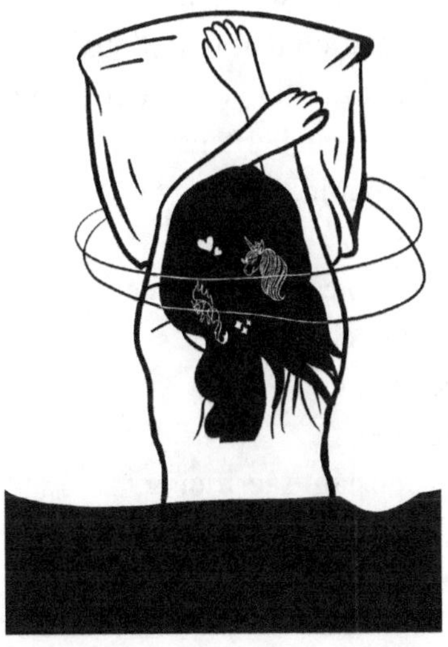

Laying on the mat in a Pilates class
I create a cage around my head,
The teacher calls it home.

I stare at my fingers, my palms.
They are aging.
She calls it change.
I stare at them ever so closely
letting them do their dance.

Gratitude.

My life,
A woman who fled from war
to Greece, to India, to Thailand
an external rotation that will probably never stop
just like planet Earth I am grateful to visit,
just like my Jewish heritage
traveling the world.

I do not want to carry the burden of
one single home,
one single identity,
one single God,
that needs constant sacrificing,
constant struggle with humans,
with oneself.

I thank my body that learns
internal rotation towards one goal-
Peace and Freedom.
Even if I never get them,
I shall seek them in movement,
in wrinkled eyes,
in kind words like gravity.
Peace, love and freedom are my home
I lay safe in life
trusting earth to hold me.

Renouncement

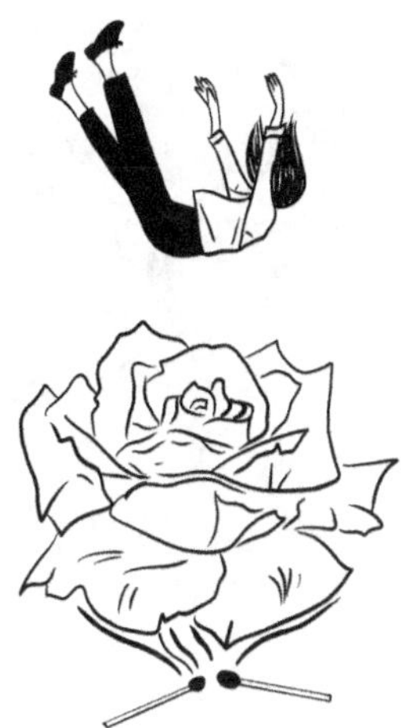

Learning new words like Cerium
everything awaits to be discovered
as we are all chemical elements.
Wind is blowing butterflies at me
all the likes and dislikes dance at once
in my aching body waiting for cool air.
Life is a mystery with no buts or maybes
it needs no "should have", "could have", "would
have".
Just a prayer as we welcome ourselves to
this moment
like escorting a bride that tears her own veil with
joy and ease
letting life surprise her.

The Thing Is

Do not hide behind an accent.
Behind an ideology not yours.
You cannot anyway.
Like a sudden burst of cinnamon
which requires a lot of repressing
in order not to smell it.
Open up,
to possibilities that seem impossible.
Learn a new language that will suit your
expression.
Run five kilometers on the beach
just because you gave birth once,
your daughter needs you again to run.
Yes, say yes, only because you can
without effort

like a white jasmine flower blossom
that your grandmother loved to smell,
even at the end of her life.

Do not argue with reality.
Not all the time.
Agree to bow down.
Yes. Bow with the whole body
in the face of everything
to whomever directs you towards love,
peace and freedom.

* Inspired by the poem "The Thing Is" by Ellen
Bass

Early love

To love my five-year-old daughter even at five
o'clock in the morning.
Even when I tell her that there is only one
mother and she yells
"Wrong! Yuval has two moms".

To love when she barks
'Move', 'Go away' or 'Come'
in thousands of piercing intonations
I did not know existed in the world.

To love even if I was not loved enough
and even if
she behaves disgustingly
in a way that reminds me of myself.

To love even when she bitterly laments that
Maya was born a day before her as if that will
explain and fix the right and
wrong in the world.

To continue to love even at four o'clock in the
morning,
Even when she does not want to come home
and even when she does not remember that you
breastfed her until the
age of two.

To love even if there is no love in the world.
There is no love like love at
three o'clock in the morning.

A Love letter

Write your life a love letter.
A bundle of them, write an abundance.
Write how hard it was to stop breast-feeding
your only daughter at the age of two.
How the truth "If you love someone set them
free" helped.
Write how "help" is such a crucial and basic
word like "stop".
End every love letter with "stop the war"
as like babies,
there is war born every minute and
not enough love letters are written these days.

Seeing things clearly—the
true nature of things

The day after Mother's Day
I conclude
Every day is Mother's Day that created a
universe.
And a memorial day for all the things that will
be taken away.

Bright Horizon- Opeka

Art, and even doodling, saves from trauma.
Meditations, and even one conscious breath,
saves from trauma.
Love, and even a frail hug, saves from trauma.

Only a war being woven through the cells inside
our mind-body,
inflames trauma, making it grow inside us
blacker than black,
connected to the crust that separates us
from the world on which we stand.

The crust that holds us at this very moment,
A moment in which we can stop.
We can choose a lifeboat,
discover the anchor,
even in a faint smile,
which is already in us.
Serene equanimity like a grandmother's smile.

Trust gravity

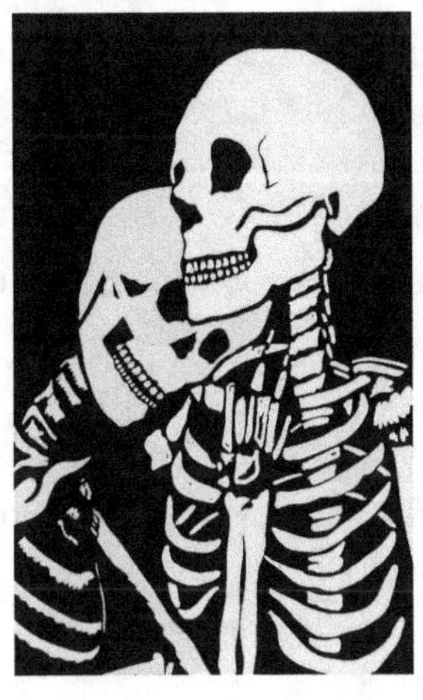

Putting on my neck the 108 skulls Mala,
from the Tibetan gift shop in Bodhgaya
is a promise I will meet death.
Today.
Hopefully not my own.
Purchased from an extremely young Indian
shopkeeper
that swore the skulls are made from real bones.
I wore the Mala around my neck and thanked
her with a smile.
Hope is momentary, yet a choice.
Just as guilt is like sitting in a rocking chair
moving up and down, not getting anywhere.

We can always get off that joyride and
appreciate earth supporting us
just as we are.
The skulls mala will remind me of this
precious human life that will disappear like
seasonal visitors in
South Goa, India.
Brief like a thank you whispered after
being served.
Heaven on earth with every bite of a
Masala omelet.
We cannot protect our death by tattooing it
nor manipulating it
like giving candy instead of change
in the Chai Shop
or saying I do to the wrong person.
Even earth is shaky, so every reminder
of seasons, of death, of structure
woven like beads,
any reflect of sunrise,
sunset is a cause for celebrating life.
Trusting gravity and bright horizon to stretch
our arms
and
just
drop.

Misconceptions

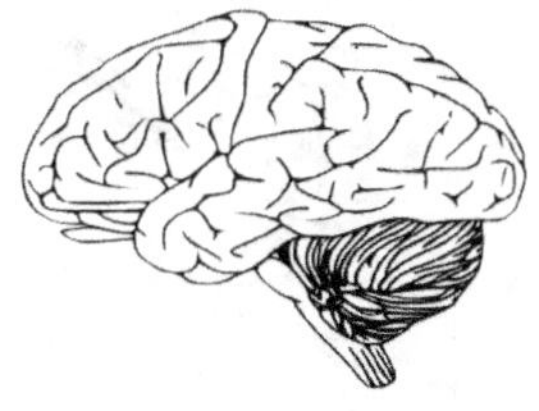

May 1st passed in India like any other day.
The concept of Workers' Day has not arrived
like many other concepts.
A man asks how they burn bodies in my country
amazed to find out we bury them in the ground.
Ironically, we think it is the holy land,
not getting the concept of ownership,
the Indians have understood so long ago.
Hold on to body, to concept, to land
You will suffer.
Let it go and you are free.

A moment

Our arrival into the world is the longest moment,
and it's not the moment to hesitate,
and no one asks if you want to go out.
Life is literally happening.
It is a moment of learning–
you're just a body, you're just being taken out.

Then comes your turn–
The great moment when you are alone.
Alone
as if that's all you trained for nine months-
you are breathing moment by moment.
And another moment.

A moment - a short part of time,
the blink of an eye,
the blink of a head that might be injured.
Someday.

Live the moment, but no one can catch it,
here it passed and moved on,
does not allow returning to the womb.
It is often impossible to remember it,
that unimaginable moment,
half a minute of walking
until after all something does turn it
into an unforgettable moment.

Your head crashes into the road
again you're only a body.

Alone.
Breath comes.
Moment of miracle.
We get our lives back more than cats do.
Moment by moment we reconnect with
what is present.
Now is the best moment of our lives.

Snakes and Ladders

Life is a game we are attached to.
Play your cards,
Roll the dice,
Be playful.
When you hide and seek
let things be unfindable.
Trust what is happening even if you are losing,
it is alive.
Gain and loss are a cosmic accident you are
taking part of.
It can always turn into love.
Listen deeply,
Speak the truth,
hold yourself lightly, enjoy the game.

Blessings

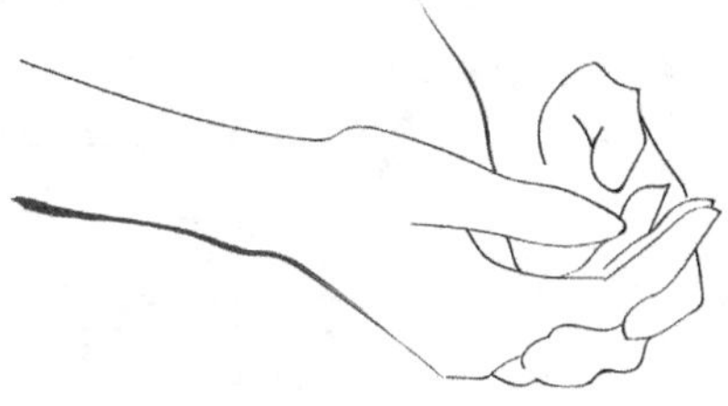

Every night I bless my daughter
before she goes to sleep.
May you be happy
May you be healthy
May you be free.

Night after night for 10 years now.
When the war started in Israel we fled to Greece,
she asked if I can add-
May you be safe.

She just turned 11 here in India,
she asked me to add
May you be loved.

Swimming meditation

Swimming. Another gift given to or taken by
humans.
Front crawl, backstroke, breaststroke,
pick up the chest, swallow water
we will do everything, use every limb, method
to reach that which is not to be reached,
not realizing we are all butterflies that need
surrendering.
Sometimes your bones say gratitude without
knowing to whom.
Like not knowing what do we do with our
precious human life.

Can the answer be Nothing?
Why not?
What if nothing is wrong right here, right now?

Only gratitude to everyone.
Only precious breath.

Everything is keeping our bones up and about.
Our heads over water even when we dive in.
Threads of mystery that will disappear.
The world is not as you think it is and it is not
otherwise.

Blessed we are

Drinking a "Guru Shake",
end of season, South Goa, India.
One beach over, Indian families having
simple picnics near a big beautiful bull waiting
for its share.
Here at Zest, a hipster vibe shared with all
nationalities,
the option to free yourself from your
structured self
is tangible like the ocean waves.
Everyone sitting with their shakes,
came at sunset time
yet staring at their phones that duplicate,
mirror the self
instead of learning to sigh from big waves,
from crows, wind and blond ladies resting
momentarily without their children.
Tired couples hoping for something refreshing

that will save them.
There is no lifeguard for the world,
not at the deeper level,
just this moment when they look,
smell, taste, hear, feel and think
how lucky and blessed they are.

Ease and Joy

Meeting the totality of life,
of that which is difficult to bear.
Of joy and ease which are right there.
Right here if we let it.
Joy.
A place where our heart can rest.
Being with life as it came to be.

Cow traffic

A big white cow and her little calf
are nonchalantly blocking the junction.
She is breastfeeding him oblivious to traffic
noise,
time,
other cows,
pedestrians,
human laws creating roads.
Only in Mama India your heart learns
from cow traffic that changes perceptions,
that lets you take your place in the world.
Manifestation of pure motherhood,
of freedom to do what it takes,
the totality of nourishment.
The word crisis comes from cross
when things, wishes, roads mismatch,
flow to wrong directions.
There is no crisis for this dyad,
only unconditional love that is bound to spill if
you let it cross the
path between mind and body.

A poem from the war in 2009

On the train home, the day after the war ended,
(Who would have believed that a poem
In these modern times would ever open like this)
The sun is setting in war colors;
Red, blue, orange, alarming black in
sunken stripes
layered and the sunset is sizzling in the
Gaza area.
The sky expands endlessly,
the sun doubles itself;
it's not pleasant for her either
to land, she lingers like a searching bird
for its correct position on the wire.

There is no right place.
She has no house, no land to which she belongs
She marks west and east and not
good and bad.
Arab female students also return home
to Beersheba, looking at the laptop
not at the reflected sun
splitting itself in the upper clouds,
it is red and visible in parts like
the number eight.
In moments the edges of the wheel of heat
darkens.
Does the sun notice it has calmed down there
below her,
that fighting has stopped?

People are still counting the bodies, starting to
arm themselves with hatred.
Mourners and one soldier,
The captive is still there.
Does he have an opening to see the sun?
Maybe a tiny shadow comes to him,
perhaps in the form of a sigh of relief.

Now a big black cloud descends over Gaza.
The moment of color red is over.
This week Jews will read again
how their God overshadowed Egypt,
hardened the heart of Pharaoh,

released them to their own country
that they could rule with a strong hand.
It is embarrassing to write poetry
when the train is packed and crowded
people and their luggage return south
towards the sun, towards an illusion
of hope..
She disappeared, must have arrived at Rafah
beach just in time
to notice how and if they return home there.

Tomorrow in the newspaper that will be
distributed
to the passengers it will be written that
things got back to normal, and it will be
accurate.
Only on one side of the sun because in Gaza
It will be dark as in the following Bible portion
that the children of Israel will read around the
world.

There will be a great shout in Gaza
Because there is no house where there is not a
dead person there.

Writing

Where did I lose my ability to write poetry?
By becoming a mother?
By coming home again and again to this
moment?
Choosing between coffee and tea?
The big hot strong coffee,
the comforting steaming teapot got the poet.
Write about a world that was and now it is not.
Write about the rushing mother feeling lost
at the train station suddenly stopping to observe
a blind man.
He waits for the train worker and lets him
escort him gently holding his shoulder through
the aisle.
A glorious moment cannot be lost.
What are the words written right now?
Will the blind man ever read them or is every
gentle touch of assistance is a poetic experience
from within?

playfulness

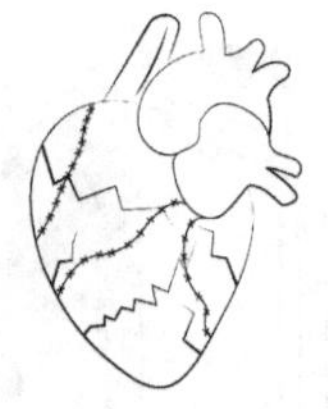

Walking on the edge of the ocean
following the winding course of water
brushing my toes and sand,
I cannot step on it.
I realize;
I cannot save my daughter from
human existence.
It was designed to not exist one day
just like the white foam that ends
every wave I track.
I cannot stop it.
I can allow her so much more,
I can pray she will meet her own death in a vast
open way
like the horizon before me,
wishing someone will love her dearly with all
her charm.
Not in my hands, my legs,
life is an illuminated seashore meant
to be lived on playfully.

Genesis. October 2023

What can be done in wartime?
Besides screaming, disagreeing, fainting,
running away as fast as you can
as you want to beg
the world to disarm itself.
It is possible.
You can still dream.
And write.
When the war broke out,
My mother learned a new Hebrew word.
Chamal – an acronym for war room.

Every house that had a missing person had one.
Chamal.
Say it aloud.
Let it rub your throat and
stay with the unclarity of how to pronounce
this word, the opening letter
CHIT or *Het*
Chit is a Semitic letter, ancient almost like
Cain and Abel.
The shape of the letter comes from Egyptian
hieroglyphs
resembles a courtyard.
A yard with Potential to become a large
safe home or
a battle ring till the end of times.

How to live with this horrific notion
you need a *Chamal* for your beloved ones.

War in Hebrew is *Milchamah.*
Compassion is *Chemla.*
In Arabic the verb *Chamal* is to carry.
Carry our pain, carry our children inside us
not to be put in the ground.
Chamas in Spanish is "never again".
Chalas in Arabic translates to "enough".
What kind of poetry can be written during war?
A time we shed tears of salt (*Melach*)
Cherish the dream (*Chalom*)

Look for mercy. (*Rachamim*)
Abraham circumcised both his sons.
They still carry Semitic letters to the battlefield.
Sarah and Hagar, the mothers can still pour
forgiveness that can
hover over our children with compassion.
Coat us all in compassion,
with kind words like-
Special.
Adventure.
Precious.
Peace.
Extraordinary life.
Kind sentences like-
Remember where you came from.
Remember you can always begin again.

Promises

When God promised
Abraham he will have children as stars
surely there was a woman there.
She looked real and concentrated
in the twinkling of one simple star.
She looked.
Maybe she blinked back at him
her own promise to the unborn children.
'You will always be special
and I won't compare,
and I won't have to choose
I certainly won't drop you.
And if you fall, you will surely just fall
I'll be there, maybe laughing,
maybe dancing,

maybe I'll gently stretch your ends
as they do in butterfly collections
and you will fly again'.
There was a woman there,
because there always was
like God, like stars
like promises.

Meditation class

Even in winter you can't teach people to breathe,
stop, just observe.
How can you teach people to understand,
to read, trust, write, pay attention.
Again and again and again.
Not breathing is witchcraft.
Breathe moderately.
Inhalation, exhalation are connected to
oxygen cylinders.
Suddenly it's clear, our lives depend on it.
Is it possible to teach someone to stand tall?
Stand up tall in their height,
in their life
stand tall effortlessly like helium balloons
reaching for the sky.
The Kwan tells us to show our true face.
The truth breathes itself.
Teaching the truth is like learning to die.

Trust emergence

Thanking the breaths
which return on time
like the books
in the libraries of my life.

Drop it meditation

The courage to meet ourselves differently,
quietly, with kind naked eyes
in this crazy life.
Sitting in the desires, with the desires,
the fears of what is known and what is not.
Mostly fear from what we think is threatening.
Drop it.

To return and drop, to return and meet.
To wonder again where the tears went.
Where are the fights, the big excitements,
the little joys,
the overwhelming ideas that come
visit unannounced while you just
sit there noticing what the mind does
when it's not doing anything.
Body aches.
Drop it.

Come back to breathe and forget,
Learn to pause.
Suffering is optional.
Why not be moved by this simple, relaxing
moment?
What separates us from our own skin?
What pretends to separate, to unite?
How little is needed to tilt our consciousness
one way or the other.
Drop it.
The Buddha taught only one thing
in eighty-four thousand different ways.
They all erupt one after the other
and sometimes like a volcano,
like a bag of M&M's spread on the floor.

Guard your sense doors taught the Buddha.
Fall down and sit down again colorfully.

War shakes your identity like a rug
renouncing its crumbs.
Sit or walk, stand or lay down
let your guts spill.
Trust your own sweat, your tears
even when they spill on your delicate notebook
creating a memory yet to come.
Drop it.

Motherhood core

How to be with all the sadness?
The abysmal, the maternal
of knowing from within.

Know how it is present from the beginning,
from the first breath
how the end is an option, it's present.

And yet give birth to the end.
And then it comes.

In an accident in Brazil or in a river in India.
Cancer or in an unmarked intersection or

in a car on the way home in the Jerusalem
mountains.

It can happen all the time.
The worst in a combat situation.
Your child may find himself struggling
with his own personal demons within him.

Hopefully you will not be alive to know.
It is not in your hands.
Mother's love is deathless.

Near and yet far

Eve of Israel's Memorial Day
I sit on the balcony in India.
Squirrels climbing thin trunk coconut trees
give up in the middle of the climb,
the trees are so tall.
Crows tear the gust of wind.

A road, a row of houses and beach restaurants
separate us but I can hear the sea,
the ocean reminds me of impermanence.
It cannot give up movement.

All the green trees in the garden
covered with a brown layer of sand
waiting for the monsoon
to wash everything away.

The country where I grew up in
is far and painful today.

I am reminded of the teaching of
Jiddu Krishnamurti who once said
"I am not Indian".
The sounds of drums from a nearby temple
announce that another wedding will soon
take place.
I imagine, sigh a prayer
that these are the drums of liberation.

*Jiddu Krishnamurti was an Indian philosopher
and spiritual teacher

Giving birth in 2013

In memory of Daniel Davis

I became one of the mother's tribe.
I slept like all the mothers.
I gave birth.
Without being special, without being Buddha
I gave birth.
Just that easy? Just gave birth?
I screamed.
I was in pain and I did not know how.
I pushed and I did not know what.
I pushed incorrectly and breathed unevenly
and no, I didn't know
who and why and when nor how.
I pushed without a drop of attention
I agreed to have my vulva cut
I shat, and bled, and cried.
And I gave birth.

Seven months later
not far from the hospital where I gave birth
I saw and didn't know what I was seeing.
I saw a mother spreading her son's ashes back to
the ground.
Out of an urn, with such jarring gentleness
unbearable tenderness, she scattered him.
After I knew she gave birth to him.

Way way back but she did.

Giving birth is not scattering your child's ashes
around a beautiful tree, a young and green tree.
You cannot learn to toss ashes.
Nor to give birth.
But certainly not to scatter.
Perhaps if necessary it is something a mother
can do.
Daniel wanted her to disperse.
He wanted her to release him
after dying from cancer
near the green tree and for us to cover him with
soil
like tucking him into bed.
I never felt how soil is soil
like after Daniel was scattered from the urn.
I thought that maybe if I touch it,
maybe if I get dirty I will understand something.
Alas I did not.

His mother did.
With gentle pats without any cuts
and blood she released his ashes,
agreed that he would unite with the earth.
In a circle she revolved and dispersed.

And I just gave birth.

Safe attachments at the Chai shop

The empty clean silver bhaji pot
shines on the table at noon time.
I wish someone would clean me up
put me for display until tomorrow
just sitting, watching night falls
waiting to be nourished.
People come in and out, drinking tea.

The dignity of having so little to offer.
To leave an open space for just being.
Empty and full like ocean tide-
Dust is piling up just like the big questions
regarding suffering in life.

What would love teach me about motherhood?
What would death teach me about motherhood?

A beautiful happening that happens by itself.
Unbearable for the mind and yet love and death
share the same thin line of grace.

Mastering the monkey mind, Gently

Thank you Paul Auster for teaching me
to always carry a pen.
"What if there is no identity?" he asks me,
the man whom I made a child with.
What if the Buddha was wrong?
What if.
I do not know.
Everything is possible-
Sab Kuch Milega in Hindi.
But. Holding on to views, opinions, identity
is pure suffering.
Gently let it be.
Let it go like ink on a baseball
carrying your favorite player's autograph.
Let it roll over oceans, parties, even wars
and you're free.

Fertility

Turn your deadlines into lifelines.
They come in every lightning covering,
flickering all over the small Indian bay.
A huge promising night of waves
shattering rocks,
protect the dancers in the fashionable
"End of season party"
alongside the sweaty volleyball players
in the annual local tournament.
Only a few cows separate the two crowds
that share the bay's land, the humid monsoon air.
So close yet so far away
like my daughter and me.

Only 11 years ago she was inside me and now
on the verge of becoming a woman as
I start my menopause
as if closing the door for her return.

Who will she learn from about being
a proper woman?
Not to choose men by their height,
To read the room, to read.
To escape a loud party, to return.
To smile generously,
with or without showing teeth.
To know she is beautiful no matter what.
To surrender to dry food, dry weather, dry skin
yet knowing she can wet herself like a flower.
Every sensation carried away like dandelions
shedding.
There is no insurance so you might as well cry
where and whenever
and how much you wish.
Salty tears are as good as it gets
to revive a garden spread with seeds of love.

Privileged choices

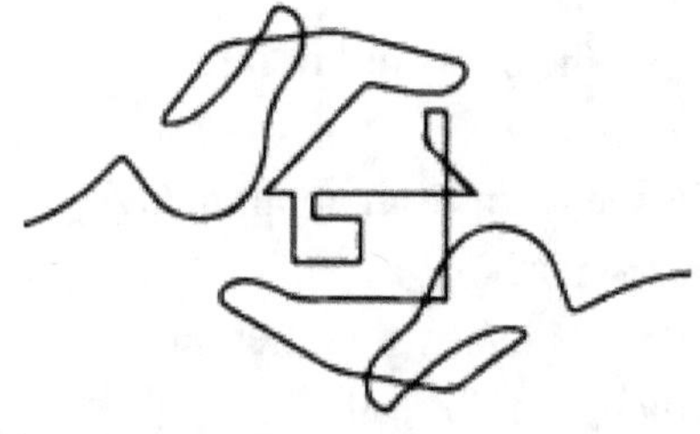

Choosing English as an
Identity cover. Again.
Foreign travelers are sitting in
"my" usual spot under the Buddha.
I overhear them talk about meditation.
Sometimes it really seems travelers
are only filling up time
denying our death that will definitely come.
I am happy when I remember
I have no idea how things came about.
How it came to be that white
men and women rule?
Trillion of causes and conditions
enabled this very homey moment in the
Chai shop.
I carry the concept of home in my heart
pour more and more countries into it.
Mexico my first love,
Tears in Madrid when I reached the street-
"Amor de Dios" love of God.

Thailand the land of the free,
Japan the best teacher for re-learning what
To do with lice in your head.
And Evia, the deserted burnt Island in Greece
gave me safety in times of war.
Earth is shaking and home is to be found
in this shivering moment.
Found in a smile,
in memory, in tea being poured.
An old picture fading on a wooden cupboard
reminds me how limited we are as
I hear the group's
leader say the word- limitations.
Exhilaratingly limited and homeless
I continue to my day reciting
Love one another- that's the medicine for us all
As love is limitless.

Standing unstable

I created another Whatsapp group with myself.
They all support Dukkha- suffering
and the option to end Dukkha.
Dukkha, suffering in the Pali language
can also be translated as
Unhappiness, Pain, Unsatisfactoriness, Unease,
Stress,
Sorrow, Uncomfortable, Difficult, Grief or
Misery.
No wonder so many groups are needed.
-Assignments
-Creativity
-Tana- thirst- the source of Dukkha
-My daughter's issues.
- Inspiring quotes about dying
My latest group and the saddest of them all is
-Reminders why not to return home- to Israel.

Father's geography

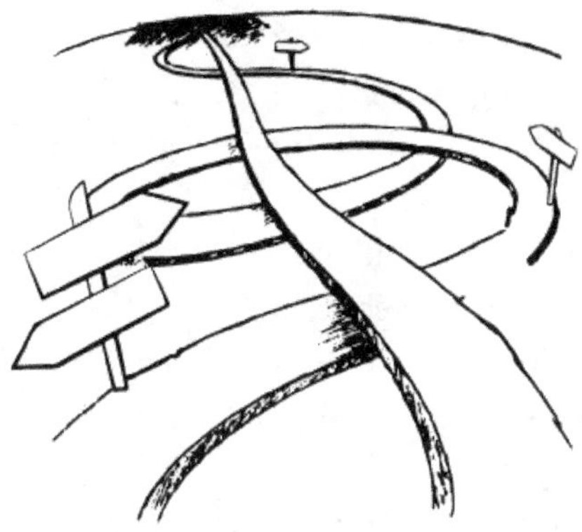

John Lennon was born on October 9th.
Imagine.
His son Sean was born on October 9th, 1975.
Just like me only in a much faraway country.
Even though we share the birth date
and both our parents were immigrants
our heritage remains so different.

Sean enjoyed his father for five years only
then he lived in his dreams,
his mother's tears, in his voice,
his lyrics, his influence,
such a tall tree, humongous shadow.

I with a father I was so busy
resenting for so many years.

Now he is frail.
His mind detaching slowly, allowing only
compassion to be present,
only radical wonder like we both saw in
the Yellow Submarine.
Sparks of joy and admiration that soon will fade.

My father was not with his parents
when they died in Nebraska.
I don't know if I will escort his last breath.
Cannot imagine it.

Our toes are the furthest organ from our head
maybe love, wonder and true appreciation
for human grace is the only
art we can pass on.

Rivers

Life is not black or white,
They are more like a river.
An illusion of two banks that hold us.
Us, ours, me, mine, myself
Us humans.
Composed of five aggregates;
Body, Sensations,
Perception, Patterns, Recognition.
Five material and mental factors
playing inside us like a wild construction game,
Oh so smooth we can barely notice.

We are not like a gushing river that suddenly
dries
we are a watercourse flowing on
earth's land surface.
We cannot point to the wild river
we are made of.
The prickly bush,
The sweet raspberry shyly growing,
Jagged stones, souvenir pebbles,
A long fallen tree trunk changes water direction.
Leaves in motion drifting down the
Merrily stream.
A drooping branch
right in the midst of the continuous flow
reminds the possibility
to soften our internal bars,
to look beyond the effortless holding
of the river banks.
There is more than the eye can see,
The surrounding earth supports us
entitles us to breathe
our own sacred river.
Breath is an unstoppable frenzy.

ACKNOWLEDGEMENT

My first gratitude goes to Siddhartha Gautama, the man who left his home, his palace, his family to seek the truth and understanding about this peculiar life we humans have. In the end of a long journey, under the tree in north India he realized how everything is inside him, suffering and the end of suffering and found the way how a person can free himself. After a long night, he awoke and turned into the Buddha. The awakened one. Tathagata- the one who walked further away. His teachings continued to spread all over the world even though they were against the stream of every culture and human habitual patterns.

I thank all the numerous conditions that led me 2600 after his time to his vast and simple teachings. To every teacher, student, and meditation center I visited around the globe that supported my path and especially Tovana- the Israeli Insight Society and Stephen Fulder it's founder led by Christopher Titmus.

I thank India, mama India as I call it for being this magical place and especially South Goa Patnem.

I thank my small, tall family, Eitan Herman for his shiny eyes that make me and my life prettier and our beautiful daughter Shira Ester Salam that is a true human phenomenon of love.

Finally, I thank my parents, Rabbi Michal Graetz and my feminist mother, Naomi Graetz, an accomplished author herself who helped me create this book with much support and enthusiasm.

I thank my father who titled me an Orthodox Buddhist allowing it to be normal as opposed to my siblings whom I thank for sharing my life with- my sister who is a Reform Rabbi; Ariella Graetz Bar-Tuv and my brother, a Conservative Rabbi; Tzvi Graetz. I thank my parents from the bottom of my heart for all they put in my upbringing, the trust, the simplicity, the tremendous joy of literature and of all the great arts humankind created throughout history. They gave me curiosity and seeds of radical acceptance to our human short appearance in this world that grew in me